The Edge of the Sky

poems by

Madeleine Crouse

Finishing Line Press
Georgetown, Kentucky

The Edge of the Sky

Copyright © 2016 by Madeleine Crouse
ISBN 978-1-63534-072-3 First Edition
All rights reserved under International and Pan-American Copyright Conventions.
No part of this book may be reproduced in any manner whatsoever without written permission from the publisher, except in the case of brief quotations embodied in critical articles and reviews.

ACKNOWLEDGMENTS

Grateful acknowledgment is made to the sources below that have published the following poems, some in a slightly altered form:

Journal of Kentucky Studies: "Black Angus," "The Wood Carver," "Hightop Cemetery"
Poetpourri: "Looking for Arrowheads"
For a Better World 2007 (anthology Saad Ghosn, editor): "Who is in Charge"
Maze from the Median (Cincinnati Writers' Project anthology): "When a Black V of Geese Flies Over the City"
A Few Good Words (Cincinnati Writers' Project anthology): "White Tulips"
Everything Stops and Listens (2013 Ohio Poetry Association anthology): "News at the Movies"

Publisher: Leah Maines

Editor: Christen Kincaid

Cover Art: Teresa Newberry

Author Photo: Brian Smith

Cover Design: Elizabeth Maines

Printed in the USA on acid-free paper.
Order online: www.finishinglinepress.com
       also available on amazon.com

              Author inquiries and mail orders:
                     Finishing Line Press
                         P. O. Box 1626
                 Georgetown, Kentucky 40324
                            U. S. A.

Table of Contents

New Year Vigor 1
Riding Horses on Clear Creek Road 2
It Has Been Said 3
My Grandmother 4
Underground Spring 5
Looking for Arrowheads 6
Black Angus 7
The Bull is in the Head Chute 9
The Wood Carver 10
Through an Open Window 11
Up Close 12
High Top Cemetery 13
Who is in Charge 14
News at the Movies 15
White Tulips 16
When a Black V of Geese Flies Over the City 17
She Didn't Know 18
Circle Above Your Head and Throw 19
Bloomington 20
A Listening 21
A Place We've Known 22
The Haunting of Our 1875 Farm House 23
I Said to God 24
The Edge of the Sky 25

For John,
JP, David, Elizabeth, and Sarah

New Year Vigor

The new moon cuts sharp
against the night, thin-edged
as the hooves of the calf

squeezing from its mother's womb.
Steam rises around the warm-wet
being as he tumbles like a sack

of potatoes to the floor of the barn.
The calf's breath meets the air
like a fresh idea. Attentive to bleat

and sway of new bones, the rough-
tongued cow licks her babe dry, gently
butts muscled legs into first steps.

This birth, ordinary as frost on a pane,
yields a gleaming black beast budding
with power, true to his ancient

Angus stock. High-pitched howls
steal across the valley as coyotes
come in closer this week.

Riding Horses on Clear Creek Road

Eager to leave their pasture, the horses step out,
heads high in falling snow. Sturdy flakes

lace miles in white. A world bleached
of stain. Only fresh steps. This softened

gravel path seems a faraway place.
We ride in silence. Rounding a bend

the horses slow, arch ears forward, stiffen
their legs—sense something we don't know.

There! You point to the tallest pine, hundreds
of cardinals tucked in its boughs. Not a flock,

but a winged city of red thunders into the sky
wildly flinging snow. In fright the horses prance,

snort, paw the ground. Scarlet feathers riot high
between falling flakes—another dawn breaking.

It Has Been Said

A magnetic force in our family pairs
stargazers from Ireland with the on-time-

straight-line Germanic tribe. The bark
of the Teuton melds on the tongue

with a Gaelic lilt. My grandfather plants
crops by the phase of the moon, senses

the push of earth in birthing beans and corn,
knows the pulse of the underground spring.

Now and then, rain or shine, he takes a day
to read farm journals and Yeats, a jug

at his side—as long as light fills the air
his jug is filled as well. No time to waste time,

my grandmother believed. On days like these,
she, a cleaner, a washer of walls, goes into

triple rhythm: sheets wave in the wind, whole
wardrobes kick and punch on the clothesline.

Flood levels of difference rise. Poles
on their compass flick north and south.

My Grandmother

Edith's kitchen table is round, ready for family,
all elbows equal. She's a round sort too,
breasts and hips brim through her apron,

full as her picnic baskets of fried chicken,
biscuits, and three kinds of pie. Tethered
to old fashioned ways, she pours lye

into water. Magically, smoke rises, stinging
my ten-year old nose and eyes. With care,
I hold the bowl of lard that goes into making

soap. When she dresses a chicken, her first act
is to spin one in the air by its neck, stretch
it across a stump, whack off the head

with an axe. Fireworks of blood splash
fence rails, grass, and shrubs before I run
behind her, grab the knot of apron strings,

peek around at flailing wings with horrified
intrigue. Not understanding why
this creature keeps staying alive.

Underground Spring

I am ancient seawater,
young water, rain, snow,

water held in cooled molten
rock. Loose, I shoot skyward,

translucent drops knot together,
gather a force only God renders.

From the depths of earth, dreaming
light and air, I burst the womb

in rebirth, pass rocks, veins
of copper, shards of life, surge

against gravity. Cast in liquid brawn,
I am elegantly pure. My being,

an ever-flowing largess, draws
savory lips to taste my sweetness.

Looking for Arrowheads

Probing the ground
with a walking stick,
she paces the length of the whole field
over mounds of fresh plowed earth—
soon to be bridled
into rows of sown grain.

On the rise of the hill
she finds chips of chert, flint,
a blackened fire-rock
from long ago campfires.
Starlings descend
to the field, intent
in their own search,
punching the ground
with their long yellow beaks.

The sun reflects
on a tip of flint. Lifting it
from the ground she shakes
away its jacket of dirt.
The perfect Paleo-blade
rests flat in her palm
thousands of years
from the hand that last held it.

Black Angus

After night has hitched itself securely
   to the ground and quiet holds sway
      in the house, the sheriff calls—

cows are out. Ousted from bed
   we pull on sweaters, jeans, boots.
      Highways and cars mean nothing

to wandering cows. Flashlights in hand we rush
   toward the barn. Corn shaken in buckets
      attracts the most recalcitrant cow. If

the leader follows the rest will too, unless the
   calves spook and run wild. Good mothers,
      you know, follow their young. Remember

the toddler at the airport who ran up
   the down escalator, her mother lunging
      in pursuit. Under a good moon,

about a half mile beyond the creek
   on another farm, thirty-seven cows
      feast in a grove of trees,

their grazing—a rhythmic whispering
   sound. Undoubtedly, cow number
      seventeen, Aunt Rose, always

coveting what's behind someone
   else's front door, pressed her heft
      against a weakness in the fence,

trampled an opening, a pass to fresh
grass. As we tap the buckets with our
hands these plodding animals

follow us through the creek, across
Route 50. Slowly we heave
our bodies toward boundary.

The Bull Is in the Head Chute

Clang! The bar snaps down. His head
is in place. July dust sticks to sweat, grass

and brow. I lift the bull's eyelid, poised,
with an iodine tip, touch at the right

moment, his ulcerated eye. Two
thousand pounds of Angus bellow,

snort, paw the ground—a seismic
tremor explodes within him—if not

for the chute, the landscape around
might be transformed—small trees

uprooted, fence rails splintered, gates
unhinged. I reach again, widen

the eye, and with an applicator
squeeze in salve, massage the lid

with my thumb. Cheek to cheek
in this strange dance the bull and I

step back and forth in rhythm
as he takes advantage of a bit

of hoof space. His fresh grass breath
vents hot against my face.

The Wood Carver

The carver's eye sees, locked
in a block of pine: feathers,
graceful neck, wing and bone.
The wood warms in his hands

as he turns it one way, then
another. He cuts, chisels, files
to find essential lines that will set

the bird in flight. He plays his knife
in long strokes with the grain, tightens
his grip, turns the blade to scrape
and cut against it. Know your wood,

he tells us, it's like human nature.
California sugar pine is free of knots.
Soft cedar will split. Tough, black
walnut cuts well with a chisel. But,

nothing equals mahogany—its dark
heartwood glows with splays
of sunset-orange—it startles, shouts
your name, sets fingers on fire.

Through an Open Window

Leaf shadows graze
our bedroom wall
as we roll away
from one another—
warm from loving.
In the distance
we hear hoofbeats,
know our horses
are racing the field below.
Between wake and sleep
our minds weave into the heat
of their run. The two Arabs
in the lead, side by side,
muscle thunder
to the ground. Mane,
tail bear up the wind
as their hot-blooded
bodies sear shadows
across a moonlit desert,
hooves hurling back
Sahara sand.

Up Close

The sight of it five feet away raises
the hair on our arms, widens our eyes.
Everyone knows what hawks do. From

nowhere, the Cooper's hawk jets
to the tree stump, wings frosted
with snow. No chance—the lone nuthatch—

flick of claw, he's flat on his back, legs
to the sky. His cry lost as steel talons
tighten around his chest. The hawk beak,

a razor knife, slashes, devours
delicate morsels. The four kids and I
behind the window gasp in one

united breath. Like magnets our minds
surge to the feast, flying feathers, bits
of blood.   Yes, we tossed millet, hung

thistle feeders, tied suet cakes
to branches.   No, we didn't offer
the hawk a table cloth.

High Top Cemetery
For Bob Larkin

We stand at your gravesite, high
above fields and woods, above
roads going not too far away. Others
stand in twos or threes between old
head stones blurred by time. Down
the hill a friend stands alone.

*

A soft breeze lifts wisps of our hair,
the folds of our clothes, we are called
into silence by your friend and pastor.
In quiet we calm.

*

Fifty thousand years ago in Slovenia,
Neanderthals buried their dead
strewn with flowers, their bones
found layered with pollen.

*

Farmers know their neighbors.
Nearby, a school bus driver eases
his bus to a standstill. The children
inside are quiet. They realize
for whom we are parting the day.

*

Standing together we confront
our farewell. A soldier plays Taps
as baskets of flowers, one by one,
are placed across your grave.

Who Is in Charge
For Nancy

The sun is in charge;
shadows man the grass,

and there is that ancient
unfurling of fern. The earth

quivers as acres
of corn break ground.

All the while,
her son is in Iraq

assigned to the 2nd Marine
Expeditionary Force

patrolling a trail of towns
along the banks of the Euphrates.

*With infrared goggles, he says
our guys see in the dark—*

own the night. Newspapers
and TV tell her of road-

side bombings. How long can
he own his breath and blood?

Each morning, in her mind,
she watches him rise.

News at the Movies

*If I had one gift to give a child
it would be an enthusiasm for life,*

said my mother when I was young.
There were no stark rooms
in her thinking. She set up what-ifs

for us: What would you do if the house
caught fire? What would you do if
you won a million dollars? Act it out—

she laughed as she handed us props.
Us, being me and my four siblings
whiling away hours as WW II raged, and

my dad sailed into the heart of the Pacific.
At the movies when newsreels of war
flashed on the screen I covered my eyes,

afraid of seeing him shot or hurt
by enemy soldiers with bayonets.
Sometimes at home I stared

out the window, fearful an unknown
soldier would knock on our door,
the only door on the street with a

military star. At night my mother
smoked cigarettes, drank coffee,
wrote letter after letter.

White Tulips
For David

A passing away causes
an empty space in the universe,
a shift in the being of the whole.

Wouldn't you think? Nothing is totally
contained: laughter, sighs, cries, the scuttle
of air brushed aside by the motion of our

arms and legs—the sound of our voices
absorbed in the drapery or the holly bush
outside the door. There is clatter to life:

the constant rebalancing of weight in the world
through death and birth. The added weight
of man's thought thrust upon us swirls

from mind to mind, starts war, brings peace,
is hidden for eras under wrap, but is never
contained or disposed. I suppose

there is a transition—the clatter
of his life has faded away:
the pacing back and forth

when he talked on the phone,
his rushed arrivals and departures, even
in death his exit quick, no time to linger

with goodbye. The important crinkled notes
in his pocket and his spring-of-the-tiger
comment held for final argument, all

spill into memory. White tulips on my table
open to a new day, bend gently on their
fragile stems, ever so slightly shift the air.

When a Black V of Geese Flies Over the City

Green fields come to mind, cattle
grazing hillsides, the scent of fresh
plowed earth. No car door slams.
No neighbor's dog barks. No taxi
or whining scooter. Instead, mist
and a thousand fireflies rise
near the creek. The full moon
silvers the backs of my horses
and the dew on the grass
around my bare feet.

She Didn't Know

how to carve a pie
with more than a sliver

for herself. My mother
of five, patted arms,

spoke of Sappho
and the golden sandals

of dawn. Her magic carpet
stories so real, we never

doubted oriental rugs curled
in front would glide our way.

My dad, a shoes-in-a-line-
in-the-closet man, directed life

from A to B with no side trips
in mind. At times, after the war,

hailed down by bourbon,
he spewed razored words

into the night, all night,
forgotten by him next day.

She didn't know she
didn't have to listen.

Circle Above Your Head and Throw

After you graze through the paper and quench
the need for caffeine, rein your body
toward the writing desk, hobble
a leg to the chair. Push, squeeze,
lead-rope your mind. Corral
yesterday's words. Curry
their coats, plait their manes,
canter and trot them in circles,
tether together a live-word flow. Then
lasso the horse, not any horse,
the black steed that rears
on his hind feet—strikes
the air with front hooves—
his whinny and neigh
echo and echo.

Bloomington

A flock of crows, quiet for once, rhythmically
strong-wing their turns in the winter wind
reminding me of a place we had never been.

For nine weeks we entrust our future to proton
radiation. Snow falls daily—robust flakes never tire
of coating Bloomington in hospital white. You

strong-wing through each day as red circles
surface on your hips. Storm-force energy charges
through good cells on the way to bad ones—

contained, you're told, not to attack petals
of tissue needlessly. In our all white world
something drives you to paint the lush, the just

right ripeness of sliced cantaloupe, mangoes,
grapes, and pears across your canvas under
every possible hue of sunlight. You arrange

and rearrange them in and around the blue
oriental bowl with a chip in its rim—
that circle of porcelain with a slight scar.

A Listening

My friend calms at the sound of large-drop-
straight-down rain, the rustle of palm fronds,
her horse munching hay. When I was a child

my grandfather said: *Bird songs are a salve
for the world's nerves, but one must listen hard.*
Still, in the throw of the day: Rush to work, dash
to the post office, walk to the chemo clinic

with my grandson, I hear the call of the mourning
dove that ancient, even-toned flute, the rain dove
listened to in the forests of Mount Gilead and Tabor.

A Place We've Known

The Colorado Rockies draw
one son to work, fish, pitch
a tent an eyelash from a star.
On a volcano edge in Ecuador

our Peace Corp son speaks
Quechua with descendants
of the Incas, treats their cows
and goats. The girls, with better

sense, settle in Ohio, thrilled
by the rush of a city. Seeds
of quiet break ground around us.
Even the breeze is in low gear.

Like migratory plovers, we find
our way to another place we've
known and loved—sitting down
each evening to a table for two.

The Haunting of Our 1875 Farm House

It never happened until our children
left home: The midnight clamor and hammer
of heavy-booted feet stomping the hallway
to our bedroom door. The original host
of the house exerting his authority? Waking
to the first jack-hammer charge we almost
switch skin with one another, bolt upright
in bed, owl-stare into darkness. John
loads a shotgun, I pull covers to my chin
as Lucy (rescued from a clowder of feral cats)
pounces toward the door into a primal crouch.
Gun barrel leading, John eases around
the doorway—fresh silence settles
in the folds of the drapes. Emptiness
pervades the hall. Unappeased, Lucy
flattens her ears, bares claws, a blaze
of wildness in her eye.

I Said to God

I said to God
a few days ago
my seventy nine
years have been
a fast ride,
in some areas
I am just now
reaching my stride—
the future needs
widening a bit.
There was no
burning bush
at the side
of the house
or white dove
above the bird bath,
just a bare whisper:
Hang in there,
I get your drift.

The Edge of the Sky

A sliver of loneliness combs my spine, walking
through high grass to find a downed calf.
Alone with the trees and the wind, the earth
and I spin beneath the bare sun.

No percolating conversations out here.
No staff meetings. No power lunches.
Silence stacks around me like hay bales
packed to the barn roof.

I listen to the edges of things—jostle
of grass blades at my knees. Lilac bough
scraping bark of a nearby tree. Keen
of geese flying out toward the edge.

Madeleine Crouse's work has been published in *The Comstock Review*, *The Journal of Kentucky Studies*, and various Cincinnati and Ohio anthologies.

Modern dance, raising beef cattle, and freelance paralegal work are part of her former life. She now lives and writes in the Cincinnati area, but still misses her horse, George, and trail riding in the rolling hills of Highland County, Ohio.

www.ingramcontent.com/pod-product-compliance
Lightning Source LLC
LaVergne TN
LVHW041517070426
835507LV00012B/1642